Love's Thrilling Dimensions

Joyce Åkesson

Pallas Athena Distribution
Lund
2008

Love's Thrilling Dimensions
All Rights Reserved.
Copyright © 2008 by Pallas Athena Distribution
V4.0

First published 2008 by Pallas Athena Distribution,
Skarpskyttevägen 10 A, 226 42 Lund, Sweden.
E-mail: pallas.athena@netatonce.net

Photograph of the elevator on the cover by Anders Åkesson, copyright Anders Åkesson, 2008.

ISBN: 978-91-977641-0-0 paperback
ISBN: 978-91-977641-1-7 hardback

PRINTED IN THE UNITED STATES OF AMERICA

Contents

THE RIGHT MOMENT

I'm looking for the right moment;
its hands touching the past,
its voice resonating in the present,
its most intense music
and its most secretive one.

I'm worried about the mirror
that does not reflect anything,
the road on which everything disappears
and that I do not see anymore,
the long corridor of muted souls
that keeps on getting longer
and the echoless tomorrows.

I'm here and waiting
in this space of mine.

I wish to find happiness;
the unconceivable,
the extreme,
the absurd,
the voluptuous
and the passionate.

I'm looking for its breath,
its sigh,
its rhythm,
its sense of wonder
and its manifestation in time.

But my clock does not know the hour
and time ignores my space.

And still one day you came.
You opened an unlocked room
and entered my inner room
like a trespasser does.

I am not looking any more
for that special moment.

You are here:
the wine lives in my glass.

OPPORTUNITIES

Light of awareness.
Void close.
Solid wall with no cracks
useful as anything
that holds everything together
like closed windows or doors.

The dust of the lost opportunities
becomes a force in my hands.

I am alive,
absorbed by the challenges
of the different possibilities.

I love the quality of the quest.
I welcome it like a warm town,
a shimmering light,
the taste of a juicy fruit,
a higher vision,
a promise that is kept,
an outstretched hand,
a kiss on a sincere neck.

LOVE AT FIRST SIGHT

He was just harpooning
the olive in his martini
when their eyes locked.

He was dazzled to see her here
in this obscure bar;
walls paneled
with varnished wood.

He weighed her up.
She was stunning;
white silk blouse, tight black skirt,
dark hair hovering above her shoulders,
blue eyes full with promises and dreams
and a smile that won him over.

He noted well the way she moved
- poetry in motion -.

Was she a dreamer?
Did she fulfill her lovers' dreams?

He came to her table
with his martini in one hand.
"I'm so happy to see you here," he said
"Are you waiting for someone?"
"No," she shook her head and smiled.
"Please have a seat."

Was she always that kind?

He sat down beside her.
She leant back sipping her wine.

She was not afraid of strangers.

She said that she loved Baudelaire.
All his poems stood out for her.
Did he read Baudelaire?
Poetry made more sense
for her than reality.
The daily life bored her.
She wrote poetry.
She wanted to be a poet.

He said that Baudelaire was unique.
- As a matter of fact, he thought
that most poets were unique -.
He loved poetry.
He thought that she was unique.
She was the elected one,
the woman of his dreams.
He still could hardly believe
that he was breathing the same air as her.

He imagined strolling together
with her along the beach,
their first kiss,
their words of love
and her sensitive eyes
brimming with tears.

Words started spilling out
like pebbles from his mouth.

For her he made music of his past.
He did not dwell on the shabby episodes.

For her he smiled.
For her he affected the most cheerful
impersonation of himself.

It was love at first sight.
She healed everything that hurt.

They traded different episodes.

She also drifted off.
She hungered for the good things in life.
She dreamt of a better world
in which they were building
the ineffable together.

Her heart pounded loud and fast.
Her lips were moist.

He thirsted for them.
He wondered how it would feel to taste them.

Their feelings were also buoyed
by the sparks that were lighting up
the semidarkness and the evergreens
that were playing on the juke box.

Outside in the city, the streetlights
looked like flirting eyes.

Life was very promising.

He wanted her suddenly beyond any reason
and the same need scorched through her.

He took her hand and they kissed.

Lost in the completeness of the moment,
in this magnetic heat,
in this terrain of love,
they were outside reality,
they were spinning in a vortex,
they were cocooned
as in a womb
or in a time capsule.

They were one.

LOVE ENCOUNTER

The unavoidable moment came.
It took me by surprise.

Your loving eyes bored themselves into mine.
I'm in awe of their expression,
oblivious of every distraction
that can dispel the mood.

A rainbow shimmers in the mist,
streaming lights fall in certain ways,
a soft melody from long ago plays,
my heart is light:
the shroud lifts.

Thoughts of passion whirl through my head.
I'm dazzled by the glow,
overwhelmed by the elation.

You immerse yourself into me.
I'm yours.

We're one,
we're fused,
we're free.

I WOULD LIKE TO WRITE YOU A POEM

I would like to write you a poem,
just to make you happy,
- an unusual one
that will give you
wings to fly with
over every defying height -.

You will fly
over pettiness and worry,
over resentment and pain.
The air that you will breathe
will be good for you
and make you throw
your burdens away.

You will feel entranced,
overwhelmed by a strange ecstasy.
The music that you will hear
will heal your spirit.
The sight that you will see
will overwhelm it with its glow.

Startled and trembling,
you will know
the meaning of both our lives.
It will move you
and change everything
like a wondrous
and wonderful wonder.

Never more you shall feel
any sorrow, my soul,
for you shall be loved and glad!
As long as our feelings
have this power,
a love poem
I would like to write to you.

LOVE'S LABYRINTH

I have kept my windows open
so that the landscapes can cross your line of sight.

Have you been longing for windfalls?
A treasure trove is found at the end of the rainbow.
You can fill your pail to the brim
and come to me from the edge of your world.

You can walk safely under the trees,
avoid the detours and the quicksand
and pass silently through the invisible doors;
- they are magic mirrors that only your eyes can see -.

You can walk in all the rooms,
explore everything that is covered and hidden
and hop through the dimensions of the house's labyrinth;
- they are dead-ends for every one else who comes here -.

At the center of the structure,
from a black hole in the vaulted ceiling,
a moonbeam converts itself into a sunray
whenever it warms up, many times during the day.

We will see various electrical interferences,
different lights will flicker,
shadows will appear and disappear,
spirits will awake and escape,
shapes and colors will shift.

Our reflections will be unclear.
Sparks will fly between us.
You can be buoyant,
I will be near at hand.

We can play hide and seek,
circle each other
or float together,
propelled by our thrill.

You can hang your mask in my secret closet,
become the familiar one, the one who is dear
and make yourself comfortable among the elements.

You can sprawl on my couch,
talk to me about feelings and incredible things,
look me deep into the eyes or be lost in your thoughts
and I will listen to all your desires that sing.

I will gaze enchanted at you.
Your look will find my dreams and make them glow.
Your poems will invade my spirit like a secret
and my mind will magnify your thoughts.

I will give you a bunch of flowers and a handful of stars.
You will give me this special ring with a jewel
that you made from the purple light of dusk,
and we will kiss
- and I will feel giddy -.

A MOMENT

Reality whizzes through the air,
smashing against the wall of disjointed illusions.

Sudden heavy thoughts,
a set of reversals and misfortunes;
intruders morbidly drawing attention to themselves;
gamblers over the limit;
abolishers of possibilities;
a conspiracy of synchronicities;
- all moving quickly in different directions -.

Serenity is snatched up by a storm
or carried off by a wave.
Who knows?

You look unguardedly at the face at the window seat.
You smile and get a smile in return.
The music drifts over your heads.
The thrill is back.
You are aflame.

THE MILK OF HUMAN KINDNESS

You let us find the right words;
symbols of the language
that make us uncover our deepest hopes.

We trigger a conversation.
Every face and every lighthouse
protects our worlds.

And you expand,
invincible presence
of the milk of human kindness.

All the disillusioning deserts,
the mirages,
the desultory speech
and the sad twists and turns of destiny
do not perturb our relation.

At night your heart beats.
I feel reassured.

You hold my hands
and you nourish my thoughts.

IN MOVEMENT

Unrecognizable climates
stir the feelings of buoyancy.

Time contracts and stretches.
Shadows shrink and swell in the night.
Lovers part and meet again.

Changes talk without a voice.
Love has a mouth that craves to be fed.

Everything is eternal:
the second as much as the sound,
the motive as much as the deed,
the sigh as much as the silence,
the place as much as the distance,
the ascent as much as the heat.

The world spins and everything spins with it.

We move ruled by some auspicious signs.
The flesh shudders under the wave.
The flame is reflected in our eyes.
It dies when the fire is extinguished.

IT'S A PARALLEL WORLD

It's a parallel world.
It's a gothic forest.
It's a bluish valley.
It's a deep gorge.

It's a déjà vu.
It's a sleeping town.
It's an old neighborhood.
It's a familiar house.

You go up the stairs of your future.
You discover the source of your past.
Your present is hidden behind a secret door.
Your space is reflected in the windows.

You find a chess game in the attic.
The formula of your happiness is decrypted.
A voice whispers your name:
you recreate your identity.

OBSESSION

The house is empty
but is haunted.

The room is cold
but is in shambles.

The lights are off
but the candles are flickering.

The bed is empty
but the kicked-off shoes
are beneath the armchair.

The clothes, the hairbrush
and the toothbrush
are missing
but the dark coat
is hanging in the closet.

The clock is tick tacking
but the frontier
between the present and the past
is disintegrating.

The mirror is cracked
but I came face to face
with your reflection.

I stood, watched and listened
amid the lingering candle lights,

balanced on legs of gelatin.

I was a free person
but a thought kept returning
to my mind:

I was no alone.

IS THIS REALITY?

Are the gods angry
or are they showing mercy?

Are the minutes standing still
or are they actually flying?

Is this real life
or a treacherous fantasy?

Am I walking alone
or are you walking beside me?

Are you measuring my thoughts
or am I talking loud?

Are these disjointed dreams
or are we outside reality?

Is this witticism
or is this a parody?

Are we playing at something
or are we doing it for real?

IN PARALLEL WORLDS

They lived side by side
in parallel worlds.

They did not have the same sky
over their landscapes.

His water filled the wells
that reflected her face
and she lit the fire
that warmed his soul.

They used to look
for each other
during the days.

She used to climb
the mountains of the future
that stood tall among the clouds,
somewhere over the void
of the daily life,
and he used to return
to the land of forgetfulness,
to the rain, to the fog
and to the rainbow.

They always found each other
in the darkness of the nights,
as they shared the same winds
and the same dreams.

They used to lie together
during many hours, entwined.

They were freed
from their loneliness
and happy.

FROM ANOTHER DIMENSION

From another dimension
someone is staring at you.
Someone is studying your expressions,
reading your thoughts,
watching your movements,
listening to your words,
scribbling notes.

Someone is keeping you in solitary.
Someone is throwing a shadow at your feet,
Someone is counting the hours,
making plans,
nourishing you with hopes.

Someone is closing all the windows and doors
in a world of mirrors
in which your face is reflected
and everything is turned upside down
and love bleeds all day long.

Someone is turning on and off the lights
in all the rooms,
out of boredom or for the experiment
of leaving a lingering aftereffect
when sliding in and out of your dreams
like a long-lost lover.

Someone unknown, familiar,
an absent presence,
a present absence.
                    Someone, yes, but who?

AT THE CROSSROADS

Imprisoned in this time,
unpredictable as it usually is
with its unanticipated moments
of turbulence and losses,
arrogant silences and overwhelming noises,
consumed truths and consuming lies,
reality munching greedily on one's dreams,
poverty, addictions and madness,
fog settling on one's soul,
threats,
thunder cracking and roaring overhead,
tsunamis, hurricanes, floods,
wars, radiations, earthquakes, quicksand,
wreckage everywhere,
edifices crumbling into bits,
too many lives injured and wasted,
and all kinds of evil deeds
against which one does not always possess
the right wings of darkness
that can enclose them
and make them disappear,
I step back and wish to be fearless,
unperturbed, light and almost airborne.

But home is far away
and I seem to have lost
both my compass
and my way.

I stand frail at the crossroads,
thirsting for the milk of human kindness
until one day I felt your closeness
more powerful than any other closeness
lifting me up
and overwhelming me
with its glow.

LOVE COMES TO STAY

Just when all the days
are alike,

when all the visitors
have come and gone
without having given
or taken anything,

a strange bell
rings somewhere
and one listens to it
first as in a dream,

then one wakes up
and one remarks
that the lights and colors
have become clearer,

a new music is heard
a scent fills the air,
a powerful presence is felt:
love comes to stay.

INTERCONNECTIONS

Different perceptions and attitudes
shape our emotions,
which in turn affect
the interactions and reactions
in our various relations.

We get lost
or we find our way
beyond the platitudes.

The view is magnificent
and broader
from higher altitudes.

The light that falls on us now
is not the same as the one
that fell on us previously
or that will fall on us later.
And whatever we create now
is among other things affected
by the way that the light falls on us
at the specific moment when it falls.

And we change constantly
according to what we do,
and whatever we do
is affected by our changes;
and everything else
changes simultaneously with us.

A fraction of a second
is crucial
for the happening
of a certain event
amidst a chain of events;
and all the events are interconnected
and we are a part of them
and they are a part of us.

THE DRIVING FORCE

It is strange
with this expanding universe
and with all the bodies
rotating endlessly in it.

All these glowing meteorites,
these lonely destinies,
approaching and avoiding
each other carefully,
moving further in one direction
and then another, coming back
and sometimes even colliding
or plunging into
a thirsty black hole before
returning to their points of origins.

Every body seems to be
breaking a limit
before being pulled
towards a new boundary.

We move too. Our story begins,
unfolds, goes backward, ends
and starts all over again.
We lose ourselves. We sometimes
forget what made us feel real.
We try to remember the faces
and the greatness that we
cherished the most. We find new clues
that make us recreate ourselves

and the others. Our life's
events take place in our memory
during one sleepless long night.
We become rejuvenated.

We go on living and loving again
because that's what we are meant to do.

LIKE LOVERS

Conversations
and memories
walk hand in hand
like a married couple.

I enter
my childhood's home
preceded by my shadow.

You pierce my veil
and trespass
like a thief.

A few words
you say
become the notes
of a symphony.

We dance
on some erogenous zones
to some Evergreens
like lovers.

CHAOS AND HARMONY

The sun was created
in a violent nebular environment
and so was the earth,
the planets and the stars.

Bodies are hauled
and protruded in this world.
Births are always dramatic.

And still beyond the unceasing pressures,
the metamorphoses amidst metamorphoses
and the lights and colors emerging from nowhere,
there is an almost perfect order ruling every creation.

Chaos sometimes glares at the world
while smoking his cigar.

Harmony frowns
on a passing cloud.

The sun licks my windows
in the mornings.

Heavy rains fall in floods
on my street in the afternoons.

Your key fits my door
at unpredictable hours.

I look at the moon
and at the distant stars
and want to believe
that you will give me
your love at dawn.

MY LONGING

My longing
slips into a melody
that is heard
outside your walls.

Your light
uncovers a shadow
that glints
along my streets.

A scented evening
knocks on my door.

Its softness
disturbs
my elusive stillness.

Your steps
come closer
in my familiar world.
Your hand
strokes my cheek.

Never did a presence
get my pulse racing
like this before.

Everything is different
except our wavelength.

Your face is still the same
in a changing world.

The clock of love
syncopates our heartbeats.

CLARITY

The fog has lost its shadow to the sun.
What is a fog without its shadow, my love?
It is devoid of its consistency,
dispersed and dissolved
in the brightness of the day.

A new season has raped
so many old hours, my love.
How useless they seem to me now
all these meaningless hours,
loaded with hollow encounters,
shrouded into nothingness,
spent without you.

Movements are now animated
by the freedom of life's tumult.

The day breaks.
Sunrays spread their glow on the landscapes.
Wisps of clouds streak across the sky.
Different shapes and faces are formed above.
Waves roll onto the shore and slip back.
Ships lie at anchor in the harbor.
Orchards glitter.
Flowers blossom and turn to the sun.
Birds sing, one by one.

A mosaic of images.
A kaleidoscope of events.

And here we are, you and I.
New sensations flow through our veins.
Our eyes are not more shadowed with worry.
The weight is lifted off from our heart.

Your smile is a tremendous gift.
Hopes are recovered.
Kindness rules.

Our fingers tie the knots of love.

LOVE

A secretive want.
Thoughts turned inside out.
My world rotates.

You're the center.

A new meaning.
An unleashed power.
A psychedelic state.
A fully lit landscape.
Harmonious notes.

I find myself.

Everything breathes, smells,
touches, hears, sees
and tastes a higher being.

I discover you.

Squares, triangles,
circles of gold are found
at the end of the rainbow.

It's an epiphany.

A non-hierarchical relation.
A reconciliation between differences.
Instantaneous responses.
A transgression of boundaries.

We are free to be us.

Fluidity.
Blowholes.
An alchemic transformation.
A spirited consummation.

We are one.

DIMENSIONS

How does anyone know anything
without thinking?

I learn by feeling.
The more I feel,
the less I know.

I must look at two dimensions.
Both are parallel to each other.
Bridges hold them fast together.

Their edges and angles
bear either to the right
or to the left.
I can feel it.
They can also disintegrate.

One of them has the bright colors
of concreteness.
The other one has the toneless shades
of abstract thoughts.

One's periphery melts
into the center of the other.
They are related
but are very different,
like Earth and Air,
dry lands and ghosts,
objects and space.

Thoughts can sometimes
be separated from thoughts.
What do I feel?

The atom and the cosmos
have the same possibilities.
The substance is seen
and the sound is heard.
The objects are concrete
and the ideas are abstract.

The world keeps on being reinvented
through time and space distortions.

It glares at us
in the same manner
as we glare at it.

The planets are living super-organisms
represented by glyphs.
They rule our lives.
The system has a language of its own.
It can be decrypted.

Each circumstance causes something
which in its turn causes something else.
The thought itself causes something new.
Every effect does not always have an enclosure.

We are cosmopolitans, you and I.

Feelings are stimulated by betrayals.
We have to stop feeling betrayed
in order to become rational.

I'm learning a different language.
I'm unraveling a mystery.
I'm using my words
in order to find your words.
I'm musing.
I'm still alone
and you're lost amidst shapes.

The fog does not clear.
The spell does not break.
The light is artificially purple.
Love is an ocean.

Can we walk on water?

BEHIND THE CURTAINS OF SILENCE

Behind the curtains of silence
a mask hides a face,
another one falls on the floor,
someone loses his head,
another one misses a soul,
chaos soars,
heartbeats echo,
thoughts drift, cryptic
and unshared,
life is taken for granted
- as it is assumed to be given
without being asked for,
unless it is asked for
in a previous incarnation
deleted from memory –,
a whole world lives,
dies and resuscitates.

Parallels meet apparently
and not in reality
and parallax is a method
of measuring the distance
to objects beyond the Solar system.

Love is hurt by our hurt.
Too much passion
can turn a person into a memory
or a ghost into flesh.

Everything is transformed
into something else:
the fire into smoke,
the wood into fire,
the steam into water,
the water into a flower.

Somewhere before the curtains go up
there is a place inside of which
every tormenting thought
is ruled out.

A mind recovers.
A body finds solace.
Meteors avoid each other
by chance
or by purpose.
It is beyond
the alpha and omega.

I'm still looking
for the healing words.
You're still waiting
for the right moment.

THE ACTOR

The camera eye
catches you.
- God's eye
peeks out at you –.

Your shadow runs away
from the lighted stage
and you stand alone
in the limelight.

This is the moment
when you look naked
and in touch
with the others
and with yourself.
- But you know
that this self
can be interchangeable
with any other self -.

You put on different
costumes and masks,
red, purple,
green and yellow
hot, cold
and in-between.

You play a role
and take up another,
and one more
and then another,

and so on,
and so forth.

You almost felt
panic-stricken at first,
but you adapted.
You held fast.

Your performance
was not very different
from the first
or last day
of school.

You talked,
you smiled,
you laughed,
you gesticulated,
you forgot your words,
you mourned,
and you almost cried.

Then you took up
an aura
from your pocket
and put it bravely
on your head,
like a crown.

Everyone applauded
in the dark.

You're loved.
You're a star.

45

PASSION

You sit with your hands loosely in your lap.
You draw in your breath
and let it slowly out again
before moving about briskly.

A face flutters in your mind.
The longing heightens your senses.
Your mind revolves around your beloved
like the earth around the moon.

Your heart and head bolt heavily.
Your emotions are close to the surface.
It is the darkness deepening in silence.
It is the diffuse light of absence.

You are at the mercy of this consuming love,
this heartless thief named passion,
who with a joyless eye,
unlocks your heart,
penetrates your mind
and devours your soul
from the inside out.

You are on a roller coaster ride.
Who are you to be spared?
You are a victim of passion's stroking notes,
a Don Quixote battling windmills
without weighing the pros and cons.

You could be talking your head off your passion.
Your moods swing.
There is no remedy for your pain.

Everyone around you keeps on hitting the wrong notes.
Every moment brings a new bleeding memory.
You retreat into your cell like a snail into its shell.

You long for your savior
like the thirsty for the water.
You are in turmoil,
a volcano gushed at both ends,
sinking into the heat.

Your breath suddenly catches on hearing a voice.
A hand stretches out to you.
You are lost in that moment.

Around you the air vibrates.
Your heart brims with passion.
You love absolutely:
it is the elevation of the soul,
it is the release from misery.

You are a hot-blooded daredevil
nearing the edge of the abyss.

Hardly aware of your surroundings,
you do not hesitate,
you do not think twice,
you do not look behind.

You suddenly defy the law of gravity
when you float freely over the precipice.

CHANGES

I stood watching
as the spirit
of your dreams
hovered before me.

Your world,
previously familiar to me,
was knocked off balance;
its fragments
gathered and scattered
around an axis
that was lost to me.

*I do not know
what went amiss.*

North and South
are unknown
to my compass.

New currents stir
your apathy and lust.

I touch the waves
of the sea.

The sky is blue
but the landscape is different.

Cryptic codes
separate your smile
from your tears.
Obscure paths
connect your hopes
to your fears.

And the sun shines
persistently in your skies:

it is still day by you
when it is night.

Joyce Akesson

I WONDER

The future stands diagonally
over these horizontal days of yours.

The gesture is frozen
somewhere in betwixt and between
reality and illusions.

Time stands almost still
behind the unlocked door
of a moonbeam
and a shooting star.

I do seek,
my soul still thirsts
and I wonder.

Do you still listen
to the songs of the wind?
You told me once
but I've forgotten.

Do you still delight
at the sight of a sunset
or a rainbow?
I do not know.

Do you still open a book at random
when the mood strikes, as it used to,
looking for this special thought,
this particular line?

Do you still brazen out the storms?
You used to clench your fists
when your principles were knifed.
You did make quite a character of yourself, you know.
Real emotion rose up in you.
You defended your views fiercely.
Almost everybody was impressed.
You could shake things up,
knock things down
and ride it out smoothly in uncharted territory
or soar indifferently above it all
and skip out at the right moment
before your wings caught fire.

You carried yourself with a certain style too.
You did knock quite a few out of sorts.

You were ready to share everything
or leave it all,
just like that,
at a drop of a hat.

Do you still organize these rites of love?
The flowers, the film, the music,
the clinking of the glasses,
the candles in colored shades
and all these delicate words
that you used to utter
on the margins of dawn?

Do you still remember your dreams?
Do you still dream in color?

I FEAR

I fear one day
that you will awake
without recognizing me,
in a cold room,
in an austere bed,
devoid of feelings.

And that you will forget everything
and even the tiny fragments
of those gigantic dreams
that used to thrill us,
children that we were,
in an indifferent world.

And that you will forget me systematically
and that you will forget me neatly
behind an inscrutable face,
serene!

Weary of knowing me too well,
weary of loving me less,
and that you will forget me quickly
before that the pale day rests,
hypocritically,
without saying a word to me.

CIRCUITS OF FEELINGS

Fantasy is high above head.
My longing is a flat surface.

Corridor after corridor of thoughts open up.
All kinds of vivid reasoning
and lost feelings repeat themselves;
- fragments in time,
movement inwards and outwards,
whispering doors -.

Connections between us emerge.
Moving points unite us.

The sound of your voice
in my inner room.
The reflection of your face
in my inspiration source.
I do not lose track
of any particular pattern.

Misunderstandings cause frictions.
These ghosts are difficult to understand.
They are born by the tricks
of my imagination
or by the unfaithful light.
They betray my insights and desires.

A few images of you
fall apart from my hands.
They are not you.

They look like you.
They cross over from the past.
They take your shape
in your absence.
I know that too.
I am not fooled.

Circuits make us find each other.
The nature of the things
is still the same.

It is the generator
of our feelings that counts.

SILENCE OF A VOW

Silence of a vow.
You kept it secret.

I can read you
between the lines.

Your eyes
suddenly glitter.

My radar is sensitive
to cryptic codes.

I think that I can measure
the space between our thoughts.

We're on the same wavelength.
This, I know.

It snows outside.
We drink our coffee.

You talk about your childhood.
It is a story with multiple interpretations.
You choose your favorite version.
You were loved, you conclude.

So was I, I say.
I can hear my heart pound.
You care to know where I was.
It is vital for you to know.

Who was I before this very moment?
Who were you before we met?
I shall entertain you
with a few details of my life.
I will present them to you as dreams.

You love the appealing voice of dreams
and so do I.

Someone knocks on the door.

You shudder.

I know.

EXPECTATIONS

The hours are pregnant.

I'm waiting for the delivery
of the right one
with the right change,
with the right you.

I feel this transformation
happening in me.
It is as heavy
as the weight of my longing
and as light as your presence.

The path is long and large
with many empty spaces.
I pick one road at random
among the thousands of roads before me.

The intimidating sight of the tunnel
does not hypnotize me.
The light follows me.
I try to understand.
the signs that will
bring you close to me.
The black hole does not
suck me into it.
My thirst doesn't drain away.
A two-way understanding will find me.
I will not pass it by.
The moment will not slip away.

I will not be left behind.

A love will be given.
It is all-powerful
and has a core.
I welcome it
with enthusiasm.
It has a mouth,
a voice
and an echo.

The sensation
of consuming it
is mesmerizing.

Your nearness,
your hands,
your glance
and your mouth.

Who would have known
that a kiss could quench my thirst
like this?

LET US LIE DOWN SIDE BY SIDE

Let us lie down side by side.
Let us lie down happy.
And before we fall asleep
let us make a vow.

Let us hold hands.
Let us smile a little.
In this intimate darkness
We can read each other better.

Let us write with our fingers
letters without words.
Let us sign them with our lips
and forget the world.

IN THE SEMI-DARK

Let me discover you in the semi-dark,
a perfect sculpted form,
warm to the touch,
a heart throbbing,
love seeping out of your pores,
eyes glittering,
fingers stroking and dancing on my skin,
a breath fueling my desire,
a tongue making my limbs quiver,
a body intertwining perfectly with mine,
a Spirit of Fire making my thoughts glow.

My infinite beyond the finite,
my center of transformation,
the elevation of my soul.

THE KISS

Your tongue
inside my mouth.

We try to talk
a language filled with
dreams and certainty.

You are a
trespassing edge,
cutting through
my world.

You are also
the entrance
and exit
to thrilling
dimensions.

I will enter them,
leave them behind
and find them all again
for some unknown
but necessary reason.

It is a full moon.

My feelings
are imposed.
My thoughts
interpret
the flowing
sensations.

Love is behind,
between and beyond
the words,
kisses
and caresses.

It is both
spiritual
and physical.

It creates corridors,
quick-sand, black holes,
horizontal and vertical paths,
ladders of symbols and metaphors,
all of them absorbers
of the intuitive
and supernatural light,
that dazzles
both you and me
before merging
with desire,
lust and flesh.

A PLACE

We should find a place
in which your freedom
and my freedom
can enjoy being together
without risking
that your light
becomes my light's prisoner
or that my visions
become your visions' predators.

We can lend each other
a few dreams for a while,
but only for a while, my dear.

They will lift us up
and make us levitate
over landscapes,
both real and unreal.

See!
Here is a mirage,
there a lighthouse,
at the cliffs a tower,
in the valley a pathway,
over there our childhood's homes,
after them a city,
beyond it a country -.

Atoms and cosmoses
will blend and expand.

Each one of us
will become a soul
filled with energy;
flexible,
playful
and adventurous
with unlimited
possibilities
and fantasies.

And we will love
each other's eyes,
laughter, words,
silences, forces
and weaknesses,
unconditionally.

AT THE HARBOR RESTAURANT

Another Sunday
at the harbor restaurant
in Limhamn.

We sit down by the window.
Our gaze drift to the bridge
to Denmark and to the boats.
She says that the sea
is calm and I say
that's how I like it.
He nods. We eat pickle salmon
with potatoes and feel contented.
The two waiters are going in
and out from the kitchen.
At the table before us,
a couple is plunged into
a discussion. At the table on
our left, a couple has nothing
to say. Behind us a family
is eating. All over the place
three children are running.
Outside, on the patio,
two crows and five sparrows
are having a free meal from
some leftovers on a plate.

He starts to talk about his
favorite subject, history;
the second world war;
Hitler, Stalin, Mussolini,

Churchill, Nagasaki,
Hiroshima and the Holocaust.
What made the Germans lose the war?
Why did the operation Barbarossa fail?
She furrows her eyebrows, wondering.
I've heard all that before.
He refers to so many theories and answers.
One of them is that the cold
was too harsh. But of course, he adds,
this was not the only factor.
She agrees that the cold can be a killer.
She refers to the French who lost the battle
of Waterloo due to some heavy rains,
- (she loves to talk about Napoleon,
Josephine, Desiree, the Bernadottes
and all the French, English and Swedish kings) -,
and of course she mentions also Josephine
who caught pneumonia after having worn
a décolleté dress when she wanted to impress
the Russian Tsar. It was the cold that killed her.

I feel like talking about Sylvia Plath
who gassed herself when Ted Hughes
left her for Assia Wevill,
and about Assia who followed
her example when Ted left her too.
It was the emotional cold that killed them both.

This was all so very odd and deplorable.

It's time to drink our coffee.
She opens her bag and takes up
the lost Picasso eyeglasses
that she found yesterday in her wardrobe,
hidden under her neatly folded shawl.
She says that Destiny has sometimes
a way of being kind, and I agree.
His face brightens and he nods.

Life is beautiful and it is warm outside.

VENUS GLOWS

I long
to be lost
in a wave
in a light
or in a fire.

I want you
to find my thoughts,
to dig them up
like a diamond
in the mud
or like some old bones.

The moment is fruitful:
Venus glows.

Spring breathes
in the new horizon.

My heart beats.
A wind blows.

I stretch my hands
toward the sky.
I pray for happiness,
for you
and for the life
we deserve.

I organize a few rites.
It is the right moment
and everything is possible.
Nature sings my songs.
The stars are watching me.

When I open my eyes.
love rings a bell
and reaches me.

The stars move closer.
I can see it.
I can feel it.

Invisible ropes
tie them to me
and to you.

A new world unfolds
before my longing soul.
I do not hesitate,
I call you now.

I am alive.
My inner light
is strong.

The energy of the colors
is in the things.

This is the place
where we shall love
and now is the moment
when we shall love each other.

You come to me
light as dawn.
We become who we are.
We do not thirst,
hunger or freeze.

We drink from the river
that reflects the day.
The air smells of cedars.
It is so wonderful to be alive.

We do not forget
a single word,
a whisper
or a sigh.

Time calls as in a prayer: "Stay!"
Now when we possess the present
we can forget the world.

We do not intend
to stop this journey
and begin again.

We have our illusions
and plenty of illusions
for the betrayed illusions.

IMAGINE HOW LUCKY

Imagine how lucky I have been
when I met you, my love!

The gods must have been benevolent on that day
when they led me right to your door
and left me right in your arms.
Imagine how lucky I have been
that they cared for me in this way
and did not ask for anything in return.

Yes, truly, how lucky I have been
that you also fell in love with me on that day,
that you gave me everything
and asked me to stay.

But it must have been important for the gods
that they played on our souls' strings.
It must have been their mission and aim
to awake us to eternity!

And we took everything
with the same eagerness,
loving souls,
loved by them,
always giving,
never holding back,
for ever in love…

And we took everything the gods gave
and we were blessed!

BLISS

Words of love,
thrown in the emptiness,
rolling like waves,
swelling in my heart.

Fluid feelings,
days, liquid with desire,
transporting me,
unclosing me.

Who were we before this very hour?
What revelations were we contemplating?
What fantasies and fantasias were we chasing?

The sky is without limits.
Love strikes as lightning does.

The moon is lit.
I can see you clearly.

It's a harmonious world to be plunged into.

Bliss nullifies the past:
my memories are lost
somewhere,
far away,
among the shadows.

POSSIBILITIES

We face the place
that opens through
the fog
like in a dream.

The path to it
turns to other roads
that always meet
through different continents
and a universe of thoughts.

We go east, west
south or north
without the use
of a compass or map.

It is the glance forward
that counts.

This is a land of opportunities.
Each horizon is close,
the sea is not farther away.

The depth of our inner force
is unknown,
but it drives us forward.

One possibility materializes
and here's another.
A door closes
and another one opens.

Oppositions and accidents happen
but the earth rotates
and we avoid the black holes.

Our home is everywhere.
Nothing is really heavy or unusual.

The landscapes are the reflection
of the realm of our thoughts and feelings.

The colors and lights communicate
secretly with our moods.

We gather and leave everything behind
whenever we make up our mind,
without any remorse.

The wind smells of harbors and cities.
We live in parallel worlds.

Old patterns fit well
with the new adventures.

We warm in our hands a few stones
that convert themselves into jewels.
We take them with us everywhere.
We stop at hotels with dazzling lights.
We taste many exotic fruits.
We meet many gurus who enlighten us
but also dark shadows who scare us.
Ethereal nymphs dance their ecstatic dances for us.

We try to avoid those who want
to steal or murder our dreams.
We enjoy many harmonious moments together.

We return many times to love's green coast.
Our pulse rises.
We build an everlasting fire.

Our feelings live longer than time.

AT A RESTAURANT IN THE MOUNTAIN

Grape vines cover the restaurant ceiling.
Small lamps glow among the leaves.
Pine trees point like fingers in the evening.
Lovesick crickets sing their songs to the wind.

At our left the view over the capital
and the Mediterranean sea is breathtaking.
Harmony surrounds us from all sides.

"Do you feel happy?"
"Yes, I do How about you?"
"I do too."

We feel linked to each other
and to all this beauty.

We eat a mezza
and stuffed vine leaves
and drink a bottle of Kesara wine.

THE JOURNEY

Where does this road lead to, my love?
It has no end.

We create our eternity
with our passion for our immortality.
Time never ceases to exist for us.
We rise in the darkness and live once more.

We carry loving moments in our luggage
when we hurry towards the light,
and we quench our thirst
with the milk that fills the dawn's breasts.

The world is giving birth to miracles for us!
- A benevolent god stands
at the beginning of the journey -.

Morning walks barefoot with curly hair
when it knocks at our door.
Everything is easy for us to grasp and is gilded.
Today's hot sun kisses away our pale sorrows
and we drown our anguish in the moon's round bowl.

In these moments of happiness
stirred by our deepest longings,
our glowing eyes lock.

Our days make love with life:
each minute is so precious
that it seems to be a year,
and the seasons dress up for us,
year after year.

We have found our childhood's attics
in which our hopes and dreams reside
and our treasures tell us stories
that our mind keeps on evoking.

We love each other's soul, past and present
and we avoid the words that destroy.

We invent a language and we discover each other's lips
and we heal our wounds with each other's fingertips.

The road leads us to foreign countries and horizons
and we see castles standing amidst old ruins.

Our windows offer us dazzling views
and we cherish the world's goodness.

Destiny lifts us up,
but we keep on falling into each other's arms.

Our nights are as warm as our voices.
We share intimate thoughts, visions and moments
that are as dear to us as life itself.

The stars glitter in the sky and in our eyes:
each star fulfills for us a wish.
We love the soft rain, the changing lights,
the new adventure, and each dawn is born
intoxicated by the night.

The new day's dew covers our hair and our clothes.
We are happy and free and are shielded by our love.

LIGHT

We live in a house
caressed by a gentle breeze.
The sun kisses its rooms
during the day.
Loving friends visit us
a few times, during the week.
Our door opens
on exotic flowers and trees.

We feel at home
with each other
and with the world.
The light smiles at you
and you smile back at me.

So close you are to me,
so blessed is our togetherness!
We live an easy life,
so calm, so serene!

You trust me
and everything
is what it seems to be.

We have believed
a long time in our dreams
to be able to fulfill them.
Your eyes glitter with love
and your thoughts reach me.

We are what we are:
we remember our past,
we have faith in our future.

Our relation is transparent.
our hands are outstretched to give.

Is it wrong to love,
wrong to be happy?

I can hear your heart beating
as though it were my own.

The loving light
wraps its arms around us.

LABYRINTH

Someone has built a labyrinth
along the cracks and shadows
outside my window.

Returning dreams.
Harmony too
from loving lips.

It's a labyrinth
in which I rediscover my self;
- and this is a complicated goal in itself -.
It is the reverse of a place in exile
in which I decrypt codes
whenever the day begins.

As in a perfect love relation
I get what I long for
and everything is familiar.

The more I approach my center
the closer you get to me.

The distance between chaos
and conflicts is dissolved.
We are on the same wavelength,
you and I.
Our love settles deep.
The place almost echoes
our heartbeats.

And this is happiness in itself.

CHEMISTRY

This flexible quest.
These hypotheses drawn
from the charades.

Whatever I look for,
your eyes reflect the light,
the speed of the thoughts,
the intensity of the colors.

All that is lost
is recuperated unexpectedly
in the rhythm of acceptance.

The spontaneity is integrated
in the tenderness of the seduction.

Delicately the change
operates in us.
Our thoughts mature
in the reverse side of our dreams.

The captivating call of Art
shapes our ideas,
images and forms.
Our glances,
words and gestures
crave its fulfillment.

Talking feelings
need our bodies.

Our desires,
so softly mastered,
push us toward each other.

We love in whatever direction
our hunger takes us.
We plunge into a heating liquidity.

At the moment when we find each other,
something turned out right
with the chemistry
and with the equation.

A SMILE

The force to construct is given
by the glare of a day.

I do not understand its lifeline.
It makes itself reminded
in a smile that lightens up a face
given for no other reason than to please.

There may be no depth in that smile
and its sincerity can be questionable.

I will know next time when I see it
if I will still feel the same way
and if I can still hear what it says,

in the same manner as when I interpret
a fresh caress,
a sigh
or a wet kiss
at dawn.

STEADFASTNESS

The shadows of the trees
have penetrated
our hiding-place
and transformed it
into a jungle.

On the wall you can see a horse,
there an eagle,
on your right an elephant
and behind it a tiger.

The patterns
are alive
and blend
with the sounds,
silences, lights
and every visible thing
in the room.

They bend also
over our faces
to watch our expressions,
study our heart and soul
and inhale our love.

I have gathered
a few certainties.

Feelings lurk.
They do not dissolve.
Between us and the walls,
they keep us warm.

The night will soon fall.
I can still listen
to your unsaid words.

An intruder will not trespass
and disturb the peace.

Our love will not change.

Joyce Akesson

YOUR WORDS

Your words;
circular as the spheres,

triangular as the pyramids,
straight as columns,
bending as snakes,

absorbing as black holes,
deluging as rains,

wild as whirlwinds,
shining as suns,

brilliant as stratagems,
bewildering as simulacrums,

expressive as pantomimes,
surrealistic as art,

complex as the pi formulas,
lingering as songs,

thrilling as roller coasters,
reassuring as omens,

fleeting as currents,
dry as the deserts,

imposing as temples,
light as feathers,

clear as crystals,
cryptic as codes,

colorful as rainbows,
grey as stones,

juicy as peaches,
salty as tears,

cold as the poles,
warm as the tropics,

intangible as time,
endless as love;

your words.

Joyce Akesson

THE MATERIALIZATION OF HAPPINESS

Cold hands.
Freezing sensation.
A thrown question mark.
A pale stare.

A warming touch
more important
than all the transits,
eclipses and full moons.

Give me an answer
to play with,
a light
that will shine in
my dark rooms.

If I am really silent,
I can hear
the lyrics
of your songs
in the distance.

You set the path
and rhythm
that make me feel alive.

I gather your insights
and the fragments
of your passion,
as the possibility
of the materialization
of happiness.

WILD AT HEART

It's an island
In the middle
of nowhere
communicating
with everything else.

A house
floating
in the air.

No sharp contours.
Unlocked rooms.
Windowless.
Wild hopes.
Outstretched horizons.

Vivid colors:
purple, rose,
green, yellow
blend in harmony.

I listen
to a monologue
through the walls.

I watch
an inner world
performing on stage.

A beautiful you.
A contagious aura.
A dreaming gaze.
Flowing words.

Which countries
have you visited?

Do you believe in love?

Have you both loved
and been loved?

Whose lips
have you
kissed?

Are you easy
to please?

You wait,
you hesitate,
you insinuate,
you test the limits,
you smile,
you dare,
you embrace,
you kiss,
you seduce,
you love.

You're loved.

Joyce Åkesson

MY VENUS AND YOUR MARS

If I told you
that my Venus
and your Mars
have fallen in love,

that they're roaming
hand in hand
like lovers,
and sharing
the beauty,
noises,
movements,
tastes
and smells
of the world,

that they're thinking
our thoughts,
dreaming
our dreams,
feeling
our feelings,
and making love.

If I told you
that I love you
what would you say?

THE RIGHT PERSPECTIVE

Breathe slowly
in order to erase time.

The light
generates
other lights
and recreates
itself incessantly.

Glad messages
fall from the sky
in all the rainbow colors.

The moon hangs
like a lamp
above your roof.

The stars look
like eyes
in the sky.

Absorb the mood
of your house.

Things stare.
Surfaces glitter.
Dust dances ballet
in your bedroom.
Memories surface.

Toss and turn
in your bed.

Think of someone
who matters to you.
Take up an idea.
Imagine a new beginning.
Follow it through.

Sleep at last.
Dream.
Wake up.
It's a new day.

The sun greets you.
The birds are singing.
Your roses have bloomed.

Someone loves you.

GOOD MORNING

Good morning and there is
a lot of joy in the air.
The sky is blue.
The room is no alone.

A hand moves
and touches another.
A whisper is heard
and then another.
The voices play together;
I trust you.
You do not keep any secret from me.
I know who you are.
I know where you have been.
I know where you are now.
I know what you're thinking.
I love you.
I cannot live without you.
Then comes the tender silence.

Outside the birds are singing.
The wind plays with the leaves.
The flowers flirt with the sun.
The streets soften with love.

Joyce Åkesson

AT THE HOTEL

We took a fast train
from Vienna
to Istanbul.

We stayed at the Hilton
Istanbul Hotel.

We soaked up
the magnificent view
of the city
and of the Bosporus
from our room's balcony
and from the hotel's terrace.

The Mediterranean sea
is a turquoise at day
and a sapphire at night,
and the city lights
glimmer like jewels
in the dark.

We enjoyed
the Mediterranean food,
simple talks,
long walks,
the silence,
the beauty,
the music
and each other's company.

- Mostly each other's company -.

How beautiful the world was!
How beautiful it still is!

We were really there!

Joyce Akesson

MOVING BACKWARDS IN TIME

The neighbor's cat
hid behind the bushes
when you parked your car.

I felt giddy
after one glass of wine.
The rain started falling
when I walked to the door.

The first thing I did
when I entered the house
was to check my e-mails.
I'm addicted to my computer.

I felt seasick
when I left the country on a boat.
My mother is resting in the cabin
and my father is walking on the deck.

I fell in love in foreign countries
A man bought me a rose.
A woman stole one for me.

In some part of this world,
a civil war has started.
I must study to graduate.

The rocket that hit the wall
did not explode.
We drank tea, played cards

and listened to the radio
in the dining-room
of the first floor.

They say that first floors
are safer than second floors.
I'm not very sure about that.
I long to sleep in my bed.

My grandmother cried
when we left the country
and so did my aunt.
I only met my aunt after that.

SOMEWHERE IN THIS WORLD

War is a deadly game.
People are killed.
Illusions are lost.
Realities are harsh.
Words reveal the despair.

In the desert of bitterness
love dies all-alone
and death in love roams
in expressionless eyes.

And the weariness that cannot dream
and the dream that is colorless
subsist in a muted scream
and a movement that has been stilled.

And not one hand comes to appease
the feverish forehead of the lonely one,
but a loving voice whispers in the wind:
"Get up, my child, it is time."

FIRECRACKERS AND ROCKETS

She remembers him,
a half smoked cigar in one hand
and a sparkler in the other.

They were standing on the balcony together.
He lit the sparkler with the cigar
and it fell inadvertently into the bag at his feet.
She can still remember what she saw next;
the firecrackers popped
and the bottle rockets whizzed in all directions,
and everything was surreal.

He took her by the hand
and they ran into the house.
He closed the balcony door at once.
His hand fell lightly on her shoulder.
She felt protected.
Others joined them too.
She felt loved.

They stood all of them
behind the glass door
and watched as the brightly
colored stars burned and died.
The spectacle was terrific,
but it ended too soon.

She remembers that she was thrilled.
She remembers that she wanted to cry.

Years after that, real rockets were fired.
Bullets hissed across their quarter.
Planes flew angrily in the sky.
She remembers the terrifying voice
of the Apocalypse,
and everything being surreal.

She did not know who and what started it.
She did not even know how long it lasted.
It was real evil.
It should never have happened.

The boy who sold the newspapers
was found lying dead on the street.

Nothing made really sense.
Many were injured or killed.
Buildings were demolished.
Houses and stores were plundered.
Dreams were broken.
Loved ones were separated.

She remembers that the air
smelled of ash and smoke.

The light was milky,
the sky was blurry
and the war raged
day and night.

They had to leave everything behind.

She still remembers all of this.

THE DISAPPOINTMENT

You come running to us
with a smile on your face.
You almost yell: "Get out
of the car, dearest.
Why are you hiding from me?"

And I already feel sad
for the disappointment
that I shall see in your eyes
when you will figure out
that the one you miss the most
has chosen not to return with us.

And I will miss him too,
and I will want him to emerge
from the dark,
from the past,
from where he is now,
and talk to you
and talk to me
and walk with us happily
back to the house.

TELEPATHIC COMMUNICATION

Surely that there are
some identical parts of you
that are similar
to some different parts of me,
and that they talk together
continuously
with warm
and trusting voices,

and that you can hear them,
and that I can hear them,
and that they erase
the distance between us
by traveling through
invisible windows and doors,

and that they inject
doses of happiness
like the golden disk
that shines now in the sky,
a diary filled with life details
or a lover's kisses in the dark.

THE RETURN

The object expands
in the remote distance
until it is recognized.

A figure comes home.
Time goes back in reverse.

A harmony is gained
after the return
to the point of origin.

In the arithmetic of love,
a familiar pattern
is integrated.

The hands are outstretched.
The connections are laid bare.

We start again from zero.
A snapshot: your face
is still the same in this light.

Same ritual:
The topics we share,
the fire and the glances
determine our closeness.

Our memories awake.
We relive each one of them.

As the minutes pass,
we feel the same:
thirsty
as before the breaking point,
breaking down
as after the vanishing point.

Spontaneity
applies to our gestures.
Consideration
harbors its laws.

Our love
follows
the same directions.

COMPROMISES

You love me like this
and I love you like that.

I try to understand
the patterns and rhymes of this love.

There was once this relation
and then this other relation
and we look at each other
not knowing what to do next.

Time has come.
We decide to part and to move on.
Time has come.
Reverse gear:
we go back and start all over again.

Again our cheeks flush
and our eyes glitter:
our passion recedes
and builds again.

Our house is painted
in bright colors.
Its rooms are never dark.

Everything of your future
hangs on its walls.
Everything of my past
slips onto its ground.

Your daily life
is bundled up into piles.
My illusions
keep on picking themselves up.

I know more about you now
than I did before.
You give me
a more resembling shape.

The truth is revealed
in our dreams and deeds.
Its consequences are protruded
in anything that is tangible.

Our emotions make perfect sense.
Our present leaves an echo.

The air is sometimes clear.

Our paradise
is constantly
being recreated.

AN ORDINARY DAY

It's an ordinary day,
although my coffee
tastes like tea,
but I don't mind.

The phone keeps on ringing.
I answer it absent-mindedly.

You take hold of my arms
and mute my feelings with a kiss.

Your fire nourishes my flame.

The simplicity of you.

Lightning Source UK Ltd.
Milton Keynes UK
04 January 2010

148137UK00001B/101/P